CLASSIC CARS
AN IMAGINATION LIBRARY SERIES

THE STORY OF THE

Cadillac

Eldorado

by Jim Mezzanotte

GARETH**STEVENS**
GS
PUBLISHING
A WRC Media Company

Please visit our web site at: www.garethstevens.com
For a free color catalog describing Gareth Stevens Publishing's
list of high-quality books and multimedia programs,
call 1-800-542-2595 (USA) or 1-800-387-3178 (Canada).
Gareth Stevens Publishing's fax: (414) 332-3567.

Library of Congress Cataloging-in-Publication Data

Mezzanotte, Jim.
    The story of the Cadillac Eldorado / by Jim Mezzanotte.
        p. cm. — (Classic cars: an imagination library series)
    Includes bibliographical references and index.
    ISBN 0-8368-4532-3 (lib. bdg.)
    1. Eldorado automobile—History. I. Title. II. Series.
TL215.E39M48   2005
629.222'2—dc22   2004062581

First published in 2005 by
Gareth Stevens Publishing
A WRC Media Company
330 West Olive Street, Suite 100
Milwaukee, WI 53212 USA

Text: Jim Mezzanotte
Cover design and page layout: Scott M. Krall
Series editors: JoAnn Early Macken and Mark J. Sachner
Picture Researcher: Diane Laska-Swanke

Photo credits: Cover, pp. 5, 7, 9, 17, 21 © Ron Kimball; pp. 11, 13 © National Motor Museum;
p. 15 Courtesy of J. W. A.; p. 19 Photo by Diane Laska-Swanke; Courtesy of Tony Balistreri/
Downtown Auto Body, Milwaukee, WI

Printed in the United States of America

1 2 3 4 5 6 7 8 9 09 08 07 06 05

*Front cover: Cadillac has made many
different Eldorado models through the
years. This Eldorado is a 1954 model.*

TABLE OF CONTENTS

Words that appear in the glossary are printed in **boldface** type the first time they occur in the text.

KING OF THE HILL

In the 1950s, most Americans drove big, flashy cars. World War II was over. Many people had good jobs. They were excited about the future. They wanted exciting cars.

Some people thought the Cadillac Eldorado was the best car of all. Cadillac began making this car in 1953. The company was famous for its luxury cars. The Eldorado was its most expensive model. The car had a powerful engine. The big, rounded body had a lot of shiny **chrome**.

The U.S. president rode in an Eldorado. Movie stars drove Eldorados. Many people dreamed of owning an Eldorado!

The body of this 1953 Eldorado has a lot of curves and chrome. In the 1950s, many people thought the Eldorado was the best American car.

A SPECIAL ELDORADO

Cadillac introduced a very special car in 1957. It was called the Eldorado Brougham. Car factories usually made cars quickly. They built many cars in one day. Workers at Cadillac built the Brougham slowly. They did some of the work by hand. Cadillac did not make many Brougham models.

The Brougham had many special features. It had four headlights instead of two. It had **automatic** windows and door locks. It even had **cruise control**. The car also had a special **suspension** for a smooth ride. The Brougham was very expensive. It cost a lot more than other American cars.

Eldorado Broughams were not like most American cars. Only a few were made each year, and they were very expensive. This Brougham is a 1958 model.

BIGGER IS BETTER

By 1959, the Eldorado was huge! The car had big fins in the back. Many American cars had fins. This car had the biggest fins of all time! They made people think of planes and rocket ships.

The engine was huge, too. It had a lot of **horsepower**, but it also used a lot of gas. Most people did not care. Gas was cheap. Everybody wanted to drive big, powerful cars.

The big Eldorado was not fast on sharp corners. But it was perfect for cruising down the highway. The car had a smooth ride. It was roomy and comfortable.

In the 1950s, American car makers were crazy about fins. The fins on this 1959 Eldorado were the biggest of them all. Even standing still, this car seems to be cruising.

A NEW KIND OF ELDORADO

In 1967, Cadillac introduced a new Eldorado. It was different from earlier models. **Engineers** created a new **design** for this car. The new Eldorado had front-wheel drive.

Today, most cars have front-wheel drive. The engine turns the front wheels. In the 1960s, most American cars had rear-wheel drive. The engine turned the rear wheels. Rear-wheel drive cars are not good in rain or snow, when streets are slippery and the cars can spin in circles.

The Eldorado was still a big, powerful car. But now the engine turned the front wheels. There were not many cars like the new Eldorado!

With front-wheel drive, this 1967 Eldorado was ahead of its time. The car's headlights are hidden behind special doors.

THE LAST BIG CARS

In the 1970s, many people stopped buying big cars. Gas was more expensive. People bought smaller cars that used less gas. The Eldorado was still a huge car. It used a lot of gas. Many people did not care. They loved the big Eldorado.

But cars were changing. Because of new laws, they had to make less **pollution**. They had to be safer, too. **Convertibles** were less popular. People worried about safety in convertibles. What happened if the cars rolled over?

In 1976, Cadillac made the last Eldorado convertibles. They were the only convertibles made in the United States. The next year, the convertibles were gone. Cadillac kept making big Eldorados — but not for long.

This Eldorado convertible is a 1976 model. Compared to today's cars, this car is huge. Its big engine uses a lot of gas.

MORE CHANGES

By the 1980s, the Eldorado had changed. It was smaller. The car handled better, and it used less gas. Cadillac kept improving the car. In 1984, the company made an Eldorado convertible again. It was a special model. The company made this model for two years. Then the Eldorado convertible was gone for good!

Many people thought Eldorados were not exciting anymore. They did not look very special. They looked like many other cars. Eldorados still had front-wheel drive. But now other cars had front-wheel drive, too. Eldorados were not the most expensive Cadillac models anymore. Sales of the cars went down.

Eldorado convertibles came back for awhile in the 1980s. This convertible is a 1985 model. By the 1980s, many people were buying other cars instead of Eldorados.

ELDORADO LOVERS

All over the world, people still love Eldorados! Some people love the earlier models. Other people love the later models. Eldorado owners sometimes join clubs for Cadillac owners. They get together to show off their cars and talk about them.

Some people like to **restore** Eldorados. First they find an old, broken-down Eldorado. Then they take the car completely apart. They go to junkyards to find the parts they need. They fix the engine so it runs perfectly. They put in new seats. They give the car a new paint job and new tires. When they are done, the car looks brand new!

Today, many people still love early Eldorados. This 1957 Eldorado has special wheels and a special paint job.

MODERN TIMES

In the 1990s, the Eldorado kept changing. Cadillac improved the suspension so the car handled even better. The car also got a new engine. This engine was made of **aluminum** to save weight. The engine was **efficient**. It was powerful, but it did not use a lot of gas. The body had a smooth shape that cut through the air. Better brakes helped the car stop faster.

But the sales of the Eldorado stayed low. Times had changed since the 1950s. The Eldorado was not the top car anymore. People were buying other cars. How long would the Eldorado last?

This Eldorado has been turned into a yard decoration. By the 1990s, the Eldorado was no longer the top American car.

THE LAST ELDORADO

Cadillac could not sell enough Eldorados. The company decided to stop making them. In 2002, Cadillac built the last Eldorados. That year, Cadillac sold a special model. It came in red or white. The first Eldorados came in these colors, too.

Finally, the last Eldorado rolled out of the factory. Cadillac did not sell this Eldorado. Instead, it put the car in a Cadillac museum. The Eldorado had been around for almost fifty years. The car had changed a lot, just like the United States. For some people, the Eldorado will always be the best American car!

In 2002, Cadillac made a special Eldorado. It came in red or white, like the colors of this 1954 Eldorado. After 2002, Cadillac stopped making the Eldorado.

MORE TO READ AND VIEW

Books (Nonfiction)   *Cadillac: 100 Years of Innovation.* Angelo Van Bogart (Krause
                          Publications)
                          Cars of the Fabulous '50s. James M. Flammang (Motorbooks
                          International)
                          Classic American Cars. Quentin Willson (DK Publishing)
                          Fifties Fins. Enthusiast Color (series). Dennis David (Motorbooks
                          International)

Videos (Nonfiction)   *Driving Passion: America's Love Affair with the Car, Part 2 —
                          America Takes to the Road in Style.* (Warner Home Video)
                          The Visual History of Cars: Cadillac. (MPI Home Video)

PLACES TO WRITE AND VISIT

Here are three places to contact for more information:

Alfred P. Sloan Museum
1221 E. Kearsley Street
Flint, MI 48503
USA
1-810-237-3450
www.sloanmuseum.com

Cadillac LaSalle Club
PO Box 360835
Columbus, OH 43236
USA
614-478-4622
www.cadillaclasalleclub.org

**National Automobile
Museum**
10 South Lake Street
Reno, NV 89501
USA
1-775-333-9300
www.automuseum.org

WEB SITES

Web sites change frequently, but we believe the following web sites are going to last. You can also use good search engines, such as **Yahooligans!** [www.yahooligans.com] or **Google** [www.google.com], to find more information about Eldorados. Here are some keywords to help you: *American cars, Cadillac, Biarritz convertible, Brougham, Eldorado, four-wheel drive.*

home.aland.net/rasman/cadillac/ pictures.htm

On this site, you can see pictures of a sales booklet for a 1953 Eldorado

home.swipnet.se/~w26312/75cad/ 75cad.htm

Visit this site to see pictures of a 1975 Eldorado convertible. The owner lives in Sweden!

www.desertclassics.com/cadillac.html

This site has pictures of many restored cars, including a 1952 Cadillac.

www.eldobrghm.com/EB/

The person who hosts this web site has restored a 1958 Eldorado Brougham. This site has many pictures of the car, as well as information about it.

www.pinkcadillac.de/modules.php?op= modload&name=gallery&file=index

This web site has pictures of many kinds of Cadillacs, including ones waiting to be restored. It also has pictures of Cadillac owners getting together with their cars.

www.1959eldorado.at/

Visit this site to see many pictures of a restored 1959 Eldorado convertible.

www.hubcapcafe.com/ocs/cadillac.htm #1950

At this web site, there are pictures of Cadillac models from many different years, including Eldorado models. This site has information about the cars, too.

GLOSSARY

You can find these words on the pages listed. Reading a word in a sentence helps you understand it even better.

aluminum (uh-LUME-in-um) — a lightweight metal. 18

automatic (aw-toe-MAT-ick) — able to work without help from a person. 6

chrome: (KROWM) — a shiny metal layer that is often put on some body parts of a car. 4

convertibles (kun-VER-tuh-bulls) — cars with tops that can be folded down or removed. 12, 14

cruise control (KRUZE kun-trole) — a system that keeps a car at a constant speed, without help from the driver. 6

design (dee-ZINE) — a plan for building something. 10

efficient (eeh-FISH-unt) — able to do something without wasting time or energy. 18

engineers (en-jun-EARZ) — people who design machines. 10

horsepower (HORS-pow-ur) — the amount of power an engine makes, based on how much work one horse can do. 8

pollution (puh-LOO-shun) — man-made waste that harms people and the environment. 12

restore (ree-STOR) — bring back to original condition. 16

suspension (suh-SPEN-shun) — the parts that connect the wheels to a car and help the car go smoothly over bumps. 6, 18

INDEX